ODE TO OUR F

All honor to the red-clad heroes; the machine

Over the highway to rescue, quick to danger's scene;

Where angry flames devour the poor man's earthly store,

Bidding to all a defiance, with its wild and sullen roar.

Some one's home is falling in the midnight solemn hour;

Now the heroic legion spring forth to show their power.

Listen to the rumble, as they clatter over the way;

There's hope in the sound as they speed on

In determined and gallant array.

Excerpt from *Ode to Our Firemen* by Frederick G. Fenn.
Printed in the *National Fireman's Journal,* February 9, 1878.

Other books in the **When I Grow Up I Want To Be...**
children's book series by Wigu Publishing:

When I Grow Up I Want To Be...in the U.S. Army!
When I Grow Up I Want To Be...a Teacher!

Look for these titles in the **When I Grow Up I Want To Be...**
children's book series soon:

When I Grow Up I Want To Be...in the U.S. Navy!
When I Grow Up I Want To Be...a Race Car Driver!
When I Grow Up I Want To Be...a Nurse!
When I Grow Up I Want To Be...a Veterinarian!
When I Grow Up I Want To Be...a Good Person!
When I Grow Up I Want To Be...in the U.S. Air Force!
When I Grow Up I Want To Be...a World Traveler!
When I Grow Up I Want To Be...a Police Officer!
When I Grow Up I Want To Be... Green!

Visit www.whenigrowupbooks.com for more information.
Like us at www.facebook.com/whenigrowupbooksbywigu.

When I Grow Up I Want To Be...®

a Firefighter!

Will's
Amazing Day!

Wigu Publishing | Laguna Beach, CA

Library of Congress Control Number: 2013922126
ISBN 978-1-939973-11-5

When I Grow Up I Want To Be... is a registered trademark of Wigu Publishing, LLC. The word Wigu and the Wigu logo are trademarks and/or registered trademarks of Wigu Publishing, LLC.

Barron Ressler, Executive Editor and Publisher
Mark Shyres, Writer and Illustrator
Debbie Hefke, Illustrator
Gina Moffitt, Managing Editor
Julie A. Lewis, Editor-at-Large

First edition, paperback, 2014
10 9 8 7 6 5 4 3 2 1

Quantity sales: Special discounts are available on quantity purchases by corporations, associations, promotional organizations, and others. For details, please contact the publisher at

Wigu Publishing
Barron Ressler, Publisher
1278 Glenneyre Street
Laguna Beach, CA 92651
inquiries@wigupublishing.com

Please visit our website at www.whenigrowupbooks.com for more information.

Proudly printed and bound in the United States of America.

This book is proudly dedicated to all firefighters, past, present, and future.

A class field trip to the

firehouse should be filled

with fun, but not for Will.

Why doesn't he want to go?

What will he discover

there about firefighting

and about himself?

Will was sitting in his classroom at school when his teacher, Miss Elyse, made the announcement.

"We are going to have a field trip next week," said Miss Elyse.

Great, thought Will. He really liked field trips. The trip to the recycling center was fun. He ranked that one "most excellent." *I wonder what the next trip will be. Maybe it'll be the zoo!*

"Next Monday our class will be going to visit the firehouse," said Miss Elyse. "We will learn how firefighters keep us safe. They are real-life heroes. Perhaps some of you might even want to be firefighters when you grow up."

Will wanted to be a lot of things when he grew up. His father said he could be anything he wanted to be. *I could be a cowboy or a soldier or a teacher. I could be a scientist, a pop star, or even the president of the United States.*

Will thought about being a firefighter when he grew up, but there were problems with that idea.

The first problem was fire. Will was very afraid of fire.

How can I be a firefighter if I am afraid of fire? he asked himself. *It's not my fault. Mom and Dad are always telling me never to play with matches. They say stay away from the barbeque grill and keep away from electrical sockets.*

Will was not only afraid of fire. There was something else, too.

Ever since I was a little kid, I have been afraid of firefighters and monsters, thought Will. *I was scared of monsters mostly when I was little. Then, Mom invented Monster Spray to keep monsters away from all the dark corners of my room.*

That still left firefighters. *Firefighters are huge! They come wearing masks and gigantic coats and boots. They run out of the smoke and fire swinging axes—and they are real. Not like any made-up monsters!*

To Will it didn't matter that other kids were afraid of things like automatic-flush toilets or zombies. Will's friend Gina said she couldn't stand spiders. His little sister, Sarah, was afraid of roller coasters. Kim, who sat next to him in class, was afraid of lightning and bugs, but not lightning bugs.

To Will, firefighters were scarier.

Will wondered, *How can I get out of this field trip? Pretend to be sick? Mom always sees through that. Even if it worked and I got a sick note, Mom might make me go to the doctor. Forget that.*

Each day the field trip got closer and closer, and visions of firefighters loomed bigger and scarier in Will's imagination.

Before Will knew it, the day of the field trip had arrived.

Will thought, *Maybe going to the doctor would have been better. Or maybe not.*

The class boarded bus number seven. Off it went to the firehouse. Will's stomach churned with worry.

His friend Tommy said, "This is so cool!"

Will just nodded. Tommy was up for anything. He never seemed to be afraid.

"We're here!" said Miss Elyse as the bus pulled up to the fire station. Will looked out and saw a firefighter in a blue shirt and a baseball cap. *He doesn't look that scary,* Will tried to reassure himself.

"Welcome to Fire Station Number Nine," said the man in blue. "I'm Fire Captain Kirby."

"I'm glad you all are here today," said Captain Kirby. Will was not glad at all. "Now, before we get going, I want to give you one important rule. You can look at everything, but please do not touch anything without permission. Keep your hands to yourself, ok?"

Will thought, *Is he kidding? There is no way I am going to go near anything. What happens if I break something? Look how huge that fire engine is. The tires are giant.*

"Ok!" said Captain Kirby. "Let me tell you a few things to start with. There are six firefighters in this station. All have trained long and hard and all are dedicated to your safety. Our job is to protect people, animals, and property.

"Of course, fighting fires is only part of our job. We are also First Responders. Does anyone know what that means?"

Five kids raised their hands. Miss Elyse called on Carlee. She answered, "It means you are the first to come and help when something bad happens."

"Right!" said Captain Kirby. "We are called to handle all kinds of emergencies—from saving cats stuck in trees to rescuing people who are lost or injured. We are here to provide emergency first aid and relief whenever we are called. All the equipment you will see here today helps us do these different jobs.

Fire departments do more today than just fight fire. In the United States, almost three out of four emergency, accident, and medical calls are handled by fire departments. Fire crews help with all kinds of natural disasters such as hurricanes, earthquakes, floods, and tornadoes. Firefighters also rescue people trapped or hurt in the wilderness, in buildings, or in vehicles. During the 9/11 terrorist attack on the New York World Trade Center, firefighters were among the first on the scene—risking their lives to save others.

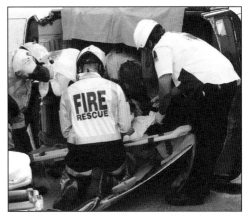

"Even the firehouse is designed to make sure we do the best job possible. Our firehouse is more than a garage to keep fire trucks and equipment. It's our second home. We have rooms for sleeping, a living room, a kitchen, and offices."

Rachel raised her hand and asked, "Do boys and girls sleep in the same room?"

The whole class giggled.

Captain Kirby smiled. "We all share the fire station, but men and women use separate bedrooms *and* bathrooms. Just like you do at school.

1. Women's dormitory
2. Bathrooms
3. Showers
4. Gym
5. Laundry room
6. Kitchen
7. Lounge
8. Office
9. Office
10. Captain's office
11. Equipment lockers
12. Fire poles
13. Fire trucks
14. Command center
15. Men's dormitory

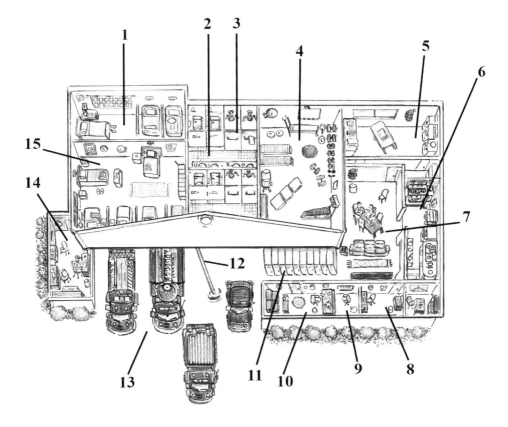

Fire Station

"I get the big office because I'm the captain. I also get to wear the captain's hat."

Will thought the hat was pretty cool.

Looking around, Will also noticed a line of lockers. Each locker had a firefighter's name on it in bold letters. One said "Captain Kirby." Will imagined one that said "Captain Will."

Carlee raised her hand and asked, "Does your station have a dog—one with spots?"

"Ah, you mean a Dalmatian," said Captain Kirby. "No, we don't have one. We have two!"

Just then two spotted dogs ran out from Captain Kirby's office to greet the class.

"It's ok to pet them," said Captain Kirby. "They love kids."

The kids took turns petting the dogs. Then the tour continued to a spot in the fire station where a shiny gold pole came down through a hole in the ceiling.

"This is our fire pole," said Captain Kirby.

Suddenly, a firefighter in full gear slid down the pole, startling the whole class. Everyone jumped as the firefighter landed with a thud.

Wow, thought Will. *No wonder I was so scared of firefighters. They don't even knock.*

Captain Kirby continued, "Did you know that a lot of kids are frightened of firefighters? When a firefighter comes to save them, some kids get so scared that they run away!

"Our outfits can be pretty frightening if they are unfamiliar to you," said Captain Kirby. "That's especially true when the firefighter comes in with an axe or crawls toward you on the floor."

I'll say, thought Will.

"If a room is filled with smoke, the air mask helps us breathe, but the smoke still makes it hard to see. Because smoke rises, we can see better if we crawl on the floor." Captain Kirby then asked the firefighter to demonstrate.

The firefighter got down on the ground, crawled up to the class, and reached out. Some kids giggled. Some laughed. Some squirmed. Rachel backed up, not exactly sure what to make of it all.

The firefighter then stood up and patted Will on the head. Will nearly jumped out of his skin. Rachel laughed.

Slowly the firefighter reached up and took off the fire helmet and then the air mask. To everyone's surprise, it was a woman.

All the girls in the class cheered. Will thought, *Well, she's not really so scary after all.*

"Say hello to Jessica," said the fire captain. "In a real emergency, we actually put the gear on after we come down the pole. But as long as Jessica has dropped in, let's take a look at the protective gear she is wearing. We call it 'turnout gear' because we hang it up turned inside out. That way we can put it on faster."

"Would anyone like to try on the air mask and fire helmet?" asked Jessica. All the kids raised their hands.

Will waited for his turn. The air mask smelled like rubber, but it didn't matter to Will. *This is awesome!* he thought.

The fire helmet was big and heavy, but at that moment, Will felt like a real firefighter.

Helmet

Full Face Mask

Self-Contained
Breathing Apparatus

Air Supply Tube

Gloves

Turnout Jacket

Belt

Man-Down Alarm

Axe

Boot Straps

Rubber Boots

Firefighter Gear

"Let's look over the fire trucks," said Captain Kirby.

"As you can see, we have different kinds of trucks for different tasks. We can also call on aircraft for large brush and forest fires. There are even boats to fight fires within our waterways."

Just then, Jake reached out and touched one of the dials on the side of the truck.

Captain Kirby said in a firm voice, "Young man, please do not touch that!"

Jake jumped.

Will jumped, too. *Jake's in trouble now,* thought Will. *I'm glad I didn't touch anything. But what are all those dials, knobs, and levers for? Where's the ladder on this fire truck?*

"The dials you see here measure the amount of water pressure. The knobs and levers are the controls. But please don't touch them," added Captain Kirby.

"Not in a million years," said Will. He figured Jake was probably thinking the same thing now.

Firefighting Engines and Trucks

Pumper engines are used for structural firefighting and are equipped with large-diameter supply hoses and high-capacity pumps.

Wildland fire engines are used to fight fires in hard-to-reach areas and are equipped with four-wheel drive and a high wheel clearance.

Ladder trucks are used for firefighting and rescue and are capable of discharging water from an elevated position.

Rescue/medic ambulances are used to deliver advanced medical care to sick or injured patients and transport them to the hospital.

Firefighting Aircraft and Watercraft

Captain Kirby reached up. He turned the driver's door handle and swung open the door. It was high and huge. "Does anyone want to sit behind the wheel?" he asked.

The steering wheel was the biggest Will had ever seen. Next to the seat were all kinds of buttons, dials, latches, lights, switches, wires, and even headphones.

What happens if I accidentally push a button and turn on the siren or start the engine or break something? Will worried. *I'm not going up there.*

Captain Kirby helped Noah, then Carlee, then David, then Tommy, and then Jake to take their turns in the driver's seat. Finally, it was Will's turn. His eyes opened wide. *Wow, that's just awesome!* And up he went.

Will sank into the seat. It surrounded him and almost swallowed him up. He grabbed the steering wheel and imagined himself roaring down the street with the sirens blasting. Will grinned.

"Ok! Did everyone have a turn in the driver's seat who wanted one?" asked Captain Kirby. He helped Will climb down from the seat. "Great. Now let's all go to the back of the truck."

At the back of the truck, Captain Kirby opened a giant door on top. He reached in and pulled out a shiny steel fire ladder.

"So that's where you keep it," said Will.

"Righto!" said Captain Kirby.

After everyone looked over the ladder, Captain Kirby shoved it back in its place. Then, he pulled open the doors to a first-aid compartment. It looked like the nurse's office to Will. Inside were bandages, thermometers, cotton balls, medicines, and even shots. "These are some of the tools we use as First Responders," said the captain.

Captain Kirby closed the compartment doors and said, "Well, there is one piece of gear in here I think you will get a kick out of. And you all can handle it." Captain Kirby opened another door on the side of the truck. He pulled out a hose. "This is an auxiliary hose. We use it when there is no fire hydrant around."

"Is he really going to let us squirt it?" asked Will, to no one in particular.

The hose was stretched out. Jessica came and set up a target that looked like the silhouette of a building, except it was only as big as a door.

"Now each of you hold on real tight and be ready when I turn the water on," said Captain Kirby.

The whole class grabbed on to the hose. Will and Tommy were up front holding the brass nozzle. Captain Kirby turned a big dial on the side of the truck to start the water.

They didn't have to wait for long before a blast
of water shot out. The kids held on with all their
might. Some laughed and yelled. Captain Kirby,
Jessica, and Miss Elyse held on, too.

At first the hose wiggled all over like it was fighting to get free. Will yelled, "Hold it steady so we can hit the target!"

Will and Tommy took aim. A second later the water slammed the target and knocked it over. The whole class cheered. Will and Tommy got more than a little wet.

"That was fun," said Captain Kirby. "But let's get a little serious now. Let's talk about safety in your home so we won't ever have to visit you there.

"There's a lot you can do to help us. Here's a checklist of things I'd like you to go over with the adults in your home. And since you have been so great today, each of you gets a Junior Firefighter Badge.

"Be sure to go over the safety checklist at home so you will really earn your Junior Firefighter Badges," said Captain Kirby.

Will looked at the badge. It was made of red foil with an official-looking firefighter seal on it.

"Now, before you go, are there any questions?"

Lisa raised her hand. She asked Captain Kirby, "Are you ever afraid of fire?"

Will turned to listen closely. He was a little afraid to hear the answer.

"Absolutely. I am totally afraid of fire," said the captain. "You can't be a firefighter if you are not. Fire is dangerous. But you have to learn to overcome your fear to do your job. I am more afraid of someone getting hurt than I am of fire. That's why I can do my job."

"What does it take to be a firefighter?" asked Will.

"Each of us has to go through a lot of training. We learn to deal with the fear of fire. We learn how to prevent fires, how to stop them from spreading, and how to put them out once they start. Some people want to learn to be firefighters just like some people want to learn to be veterinarians. Everyone is different."

Will thought, *I could be a firefighter if I wanted to*.

Then Will put on his Junior Firefighter Badge. "I can do this," he said out loud.

Will looked up from his badge when Miss Elyse announced that the tour was over. *What? How can it be over so soon?* he thought.

Throughout the rest of the day and all the way up until bedtime, Will thought about everything he had learned about being a firefighter.

That night, Will sat in bed, looking at his Junior Firefighter Badge and checklist. "Tomorrow, I'm going to go through my house to make sure it is safe."

Putting his head on his pillow, Will thought about his day. He thought about the fire pole, the air mask, the fire helmet, and the hose. He thought about the truck and sitting in the driver's seat. Going to the firehouse had been a "most excellent" field trip after all!

Will knew now he was no longer going to be afraid of firefighters. He discovered today, to his surprise, that even firefighters and fire captains could be just as afraid of fire as he was.

And he knew one more thing.

Yeah—I know I really want to be a firefighter when I grow up!

As Will closed his eyes, he smiled at the thought.

Then he fell asleep and dreamed.

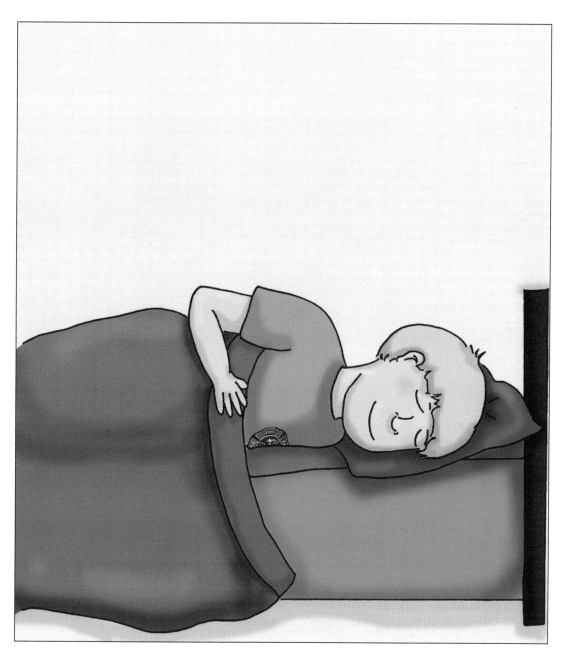

HOME FIRE SAFETY CHECKLIST
A Guide to Fire Prevention

Kitchen Safety
Make sure:

- ✔ A grown-up is always in the kitchen when food is cooking on the stove.
- ✔ Stove tops and counters are clean and uncluttered.
- ✔ Curtains and other things that can burn are far away from the stove.

Heating Safety
Make sure:

- ✔ Portable space heaters are always turned off when an adult leaves the room or goes to sleep.
- ✔ Space heaters are at least three feet away from anything that can burn, like people, pets, and furniture.
- ✔ Fireplaces have sturdy screens to catch sparks.

Electrical Safety
Make sure:

- ✔ Extension cords are used safely and are never under carpets or across doorways.
- ✔ Electrical cords are in good condition without cracks or frayed areas.
- ✔ Kitchen appliances such as coffee-makers and toaster ovens are plugged into separate outlets.

Smoke Alarms/Home Fire Escape
Make sure:

- ✔ Your home has working smoke alarms on every level.
- ✔ All home exits are clear of furniture, toys, and clutter.
- ✔ Your family has a Home Fire Escape Plan.
- ✔ Your whole family practices home fire drills.
- ✔ You know the fire department's emergency phone number.

Draw a map of your home using a piece of paper. Show all doors and windows.
Visit each room. Find two ways out.

All windows and doors should open easily. You should be able to use them to get outside.

Make sure your home has smoke alarms. Push the test button to make sure each alarm is working.

Pick a meeting place outside. It should be in front of your home. Everyone will meet at the meeting place.

Make sure your house or building number can be seen from the street.

Talk about your plan with everyone in your home.

Learn the emergency phone number for your fire department.

Practice your home fire escape drill!

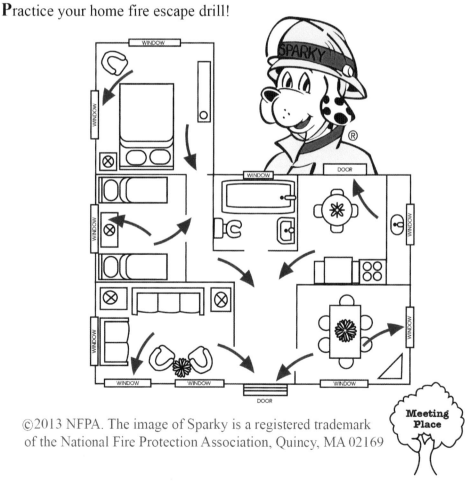

9407351R00035

Made in the USA
San Bernardino, CA
14 March 2014